Dorothy Scheuer

SCHOLASTIC BOOK SERVICES
New York Toronto London Auckland Sydney Tokyo

Grateful acknowledgment for their assistance in the preparation of this book is made to: ABC-TV, The Blake Agency, CBS-TV, Lucy Evankow, Hanson & Schwam Public Relations, ICPR Public Relations, MGM-TV, MTM Enterprises, NBC-TV, Paramount Television, Rogers & Cowan Public Relations, David T. Scheuer, Helene E. Schwartz, Tandem/T.A.T. Productions, 20th Century-Fox Television, Warner Bros. Television.

ISBN 0-590-32340-7

12 11 10 9 8 7 6 5 4 3 2 1   1   2 3 4 5 6 7/8

for Shirley E.

THE GREATEST AMERICAN HERO

(ABC)

Is he faster than a speeding bullet?
Yes, but he's often going in the wrong direction.
Is he more powerful than a locomotive?
Sure, but once he grabs hold of the getaway car, he's not
sure about what to do with the crooks inside.
Can he leap tall buildings at a single bound?
Of course, unless he trips over the guardrail on the roof.
Who is he? Ralph. A mild-mannered high school teacher.
Until last spring, his biggest problem was getting his students
to settle down in class. Then he happened to encounter some
aliens on a dark night in the desert. The aliens gave him a box;
inside it was a suit that would give Ralph superpowers. Ralph's
mission—should FBI agent Bill Maxwell be able to convince
him to accept it—was this: Save the country from crime and
corruption. "Why me?" Ralph yelped. He promptly lost the
instruction booklet that explained how to use his new powers.
The latest American hero was born.

William Katt

William Katt was born on February 16. The son of actors
Barbara Hale (Della Street on *Perry Mason*) and Bill Williams
(who played the title role in the *Kit Carson* series), he grew
up next door to Tom Selleck, now star of *Magnum, P.I.*

Bill's character, Ralph, wasn't sure he wanted to become a hero. Katt himself wasn't sure about becoming an actor. He'd done some theater and TV work while in school, but he didn't think of it as a career; at the time he was more interested in music. Then he took the role of Sissy Spacek's prom date in *Carrie*. The reaction of movie audiences was so positive that Bill started taking acting seriously.

He had roles in two more feature films: *First Love* with Susan Dey, and *Big Wednesday* with Jan-Michael Vincent and Gary Busey. Then he starred in the TV movie *Butch and Sundance: The Early Years*. None of these were as successful as *Carrie,* and Bill went back to the theater until he was offered the role in the TV series *The Greatest American Hero*.

Bill has two sisters, one older and one younger than he is. He is married, and he and his wife, Debbie, have a young son, Clayton.

Connie Sellecca

Connie Sellecca, who plays Ralph's friend and lawyer, Pam, didn't like what she saw in the mirror. During junior high school, she says, "I was very unattractive. I had a mouth full of braces, very thick glasses, and long stringy hair." But Connie blossomed during high school and went straight from graduation into a successful modeling career. She'd acted in some high school plays, and in 1977 she moved to TV movies with *The Bermuda Depths*. After that came the series *Flying High*.

Connie has appeared in the TV movies *She's Dressed to Kill* and *Captain America,* and in the series *Beyond Westworld*. She's married to Gil Gerard (TV's Buck Rogers), whom she met on an airplane. They live in California with their two dogs.

Robert Culp

Robert Culp's character, FBI agent Bill Maxwell, is charged with overseeing Ralph's superhero activities. Culp has experience as a mastermind, being an actor, writer, director, and producer. He put most of those talents to work in his first big series, *I Spy,* with Bill Cosby.

Culp has written plays,and he produced the TV documentary *Operation Breadbasket,* a study of black economics. He has also written TV scripts, including the pilot for *I Spy.*

A star athlete, Culp turned down six athletic scholarship offers in favor of studying theater arts in college. He has appeared in the films *PT 109* and *Bob and Carol and Ted and Alice,* and on TV in *Police Story* and *Roots: The Next Generations.*

You can write to the stars of *The Greatest American Hero* at:

The Greatest American Hero
% Stephen J. Cannell Productions
5451 Marathon Street
Los Angeles, CA 90038

THE DUKES OF HAZZARD (CBS)

Anyone can tell you—if you don't already know—that *The Dukes of Hazzard* is one of the most popular shows on TV. It started off on top, back in January 1979. That's when the Duke cousins first drove the General Lee over the country roads of Hazzard County. Besides the fun-loving Duke family, this fictional Southern community has a corrupt local politician named Jefferson Davis ("Boss") Hogg. Every week the Dukes find themselves in trouble with Boss Hogg's version of the law, but they always manage to prove their innocence in the end.

What makes this show so popular? Two answers high on the list are plenty of fast action and the show's four bright new stars: the three Duke cousins, Bo, Luke, and Daisy—played by John Schneider, Tom Wopat, and Catherine Bach—and the General Lee, their fiery red car.

The General Lee has been through a lot with the Dukes; in fact, the Dukes have actually gone through several General Lees. The wild stunts Bo and Luke execute with their trusty wheels are more than any one car can take, and in a single episode you may actually be seeing more than one specially painted 1969 Dodge Charger with the "01" insignia. When one needs repairs, part are borrowed from another. The original General Lee is still in use on the show—and still in flawless condition. That's because you only see it in the straight driving scenes: the "stand-ins" do all the stunts.

John Schneider

John Schneider is the original blond 'n' blue-eyed Bo Duke. John really is an expert driver, and he loves being behind the wheel of the General Lee. But he's a guy with many other talents as well.

First, the vital statistics. John was born in Mt. Kisco, New York, on April 8, two years before his parents were divorced. After the breakup, John went to live with his mom, and he went with her when she took a job in Atlanta, Georgia. John's brother Bob stayed behind with their dad, who had remarried.

Atlanta had a strong community theater, and John quickly became active in both school and community dramatics. He appeared in *Fiddler on the Roof, Annie Get Your Gun, The Wizard of Oz,* and many other productions. He has also performed in summer stock (in New Hampshire) in the musical *Bye Bye Birdie,* and off-Broadway (in New York) in *Li'l Abner.*

In addition to his acting, John learned to play the guitar and accompanied himself singing his own songs in Atlanta nightclubs. He also learned a bagful of magician's tricks and performed his sleight-of-hand at private parties. John's musical and magical talents were displayed in a TV special last season, *Back Home with John Schneider.* His first LP, "It's Now or Never," was released last spring.

The shy grin John flashes on the fan magazine covers almost every month might make you think he's a pussycat. And it's true that a lot of people meeting him for the first time are impressed by his warm, gentle manner. But John also has a lot of determination, and he knows how to get what he wants.

One example of this is the way he took off almost fifty pounds when he was an overweight teenager. According to John, all it took was "willpower" and the encouragement of someone who cared—in this case, his brother Bob. But if you've ever tried to change something about yourself, you know how big an effort it can take.

Another example is the way John got the role of Bo Duke. The call came for a natural, good ol' country boy, not much experience required. John strolled into the interview wearing casual clothes and affecting a strong Southern twang in his voice. It wasn't until after he'd gotten the job that his co-workers found out he'd *really* grown up in the North and in a big Southern *city,* and that he had plenty of acting credentials.

But nobody minded for long. John helped to make *The Dukes of Hazzard* an enormous television success. And all you have to do is watch him to know that he's perfect for the part.

Tom Wopat

Tom Wopat didn't decide he wanted to be an actor until he got to high school. Growing up in Lodi, Wisconsin, he had other things on his mind. Cows, for one. Tom's parents ran -

a dairy farm, and every day before school, Tom would get up early to help with the milking.

It wasn't lonely at the crack of dawn: Tom had his six brothers and a sister to keep him company. Four brothers are older than Tom; the other two and his sister are younger. Tom's birthday is September 9.

Even when he got to high school, Tom had other interests besides acting. He plays the guitar and trombone and he was in a band, the school chorus, and on the football and track teams. In his spare time, Tom still likes to play football—and basketball, softball, and Frisbee.

For a long while, it looked like Tom might pursue a career in music, and in fact, he is still working on getting a recording contract. He studied music in college, at the University of Wisconsin. He has a degree in applied voice, and his strong tenor voice once even won him an opera audition. For a year and a half, Tom was lead singer and trombone player for a rock band called Skyway. But he likes lots of different kinds of music. "The only music I don't really like at all is hard rock," he says.

It makes sense that when Tom did turn to acting, he specialized in musicals. He's appeared on stage in *The Pajama Game* and *Annie Get Your Gun*, and he has played the lead in *Oklahoma!* Tom's also been in *Equus, The Robber Bridegroom*, and, on Broadway in New York, he had a starring role in the musical comedy *I Love My Wife*.

Tom's first TV role was a short run in the ABC daytime drama *One Life to Live*. His second? The part of Luke Duke.

With all of his many talents — and in spite of growing up in a big family — Tom still managed to become a shy fellow. The hit TV series he's in has helped him come out of his shell and feel more comfortable with people, but he still has a quiet side. It's that quiet side that helps make Luke Duke seem so thoughtful and appealing. But neither Tom nor Luke is the kind to hide in a corner. Tom's favorite part of the show is the action, and one of his favorite ways to relax off-screen is to climb on his Yamaha 650 motorcycle and take an exhilarating ride. His tamer hobbies include playing guitar and listening to music.

Tom thinks the best preparation for a career in show business is to learn to do a lot of different things. Even if you plan to be an actor, he says, you should be able to sing and dance. Playing a musical instrument or two can't hurt, either. Tom ought to know. That's how *he* did it!

Catherine Bach

Daisy Duke was criticized for her skimpy costumes when *The Dukes* first began, but Cathy Bach has turned her character into more than just a pretty pair of legs. The waitress at Boss Hogg's roadhouse is smart, brave in difficult situations, and genuinely friendly to the men *and* women who pass through Hazzard County.

"Daisy's a lot of real people rolled into one," Cathy says.

"She's part the wildest girl I knew in high school, and part some friends I had in Georgia. There's some of Dolly Parton in her, and a lot of *me* from when I was a waitress in real life."

Cathy really is a country girl. She was born in Warren, Ohio, and spent her years as a teenager on her dad's ranch in Faith, South Dakota. In between, her parents were divorced, and for a while Cathy lived with her Mexican mom in Los Angeles. Back on the ranch, she studied ballet and became a high school track star. But Cathy dreamed of returning to L.A. and pursuing a career in acting. So she took a job in the soda fountain of the local Woolworth's and started saving for a plane ticket. Dad did not approve of his daughter's ambitions, but by the time Cathy was seventeen, she had enough money saved to put her dreams into action.

Los Angeles is one of the best places to be if you want to get into acting, but the competition is stiff. Cathy did get a few roles in small theater productions, but most of her income came from her job as a legal secretary. In 1974, she got a small part in the movie *Thunderbolt and Lightfoot,* and in 1975 she had another tiny role in the movie *Hustle.* She also made TV guest appearances, in such series as *Police Story, Matt Helm, Strange New World,* and *Police Woman.*

In 1976, Cathy met theatrical manager David Shaw. After a three-month courtship, they got married. (They later separated.) Shaw had a friend who was writing a pilot for a new series; he met Cathy and decided she was perfect for a part in it. The show's title? *The Dukes of Hazzard.*

These days Cathy's life is as hectic off-screen as Daisy Duke's is on. Her "free" time is jammed full of charity work, traveling, horseback riding, reading, dancing (jazz and disco), and playing the piano. She loves to sing and would like a recording career someday. Cathy often appears on television specials such as *Battle of the Network Stars,* and when 1979 became 1980, Cathy climbed atop a tower at Times Square in New York and — on national television — helped usher in the new year.

Cathy loves to get mail, and she and her mom answer as many letters as they can. There's lots of it, so be patient! (The address for Cathy and the other *Dukes* stars appears at the end of the chapter.)

Of course, there are more characters in Hazzard County than the Duke cousins. Do you know these facts about the actors who play them?

Sorrell Booke
Without Boss Hogg to complicate their lives, the Dukes wouldn't have much to do besides ride around in General Lee. Sorrell Booke, who plays the cantankerous old coot, is actually a highly educated man who speaks half a dozen languages. He's had parts in more than 150 TV series, starting with *Route 66* and including *Soap* and *What's Happening!!* His twenty feature film roles include *What's Up Doc?* and *Freaky Friday*.

James Best
Now, Boss Hogg would never soil his pretty white suit by doing his own dirty work. That's why he has his brother-in-law, the slightly inept Sheriff Roscoe P. Coltrane, played by James Best. But Best is a lot more competent than his on-screen character. He has taught, acted, and directed plays at the University of Mississippi; and he was founder of both the Mississippi Film Commission and the Mississippi Ballet Theater. He's written four screenplays and thirty stage plays, and seven of his songs have been recorded. Best's first movie was *Comanche Territory*, in 1949; more recently, he had roles in *Sounder* and *Hooper*.

Denver Pyle
The small-town atmosphere of Hazzard County makes Denver Pyle (Uncle Jesse) feel right at home. He grew up in a

small Colorado town — population: forty. The Duke cousins' genial uncle fits right into country living, but Pyle is just as comfortable on the water, in his fifty-foot cabin cruiser. Pyle's been appearing on television since its earliest series — especially in Westerns — and his last regular role before *The Dukes of Hazzard* was as Mad Jack on *The Life and Times of Grizzly Adams*.

Ben Jones

Ben Jones (Cooter) is another real-life small-town fellow. "I don't like staying in big cities any longer than necessary," he says. Jones has been in fifty commercials, and he's traveled across the country in a one-man show for children that he also wrote, directed, and produced.

Rick Hurst

Cletus — Roscoe's deputy and Boss Hogg's country cousin — became a regular character on *The Dukes of Hazzard* last season when Sonny Shroyer left to do its spin-off, *Enos*. Before creating the role, Rick Hurst concentrated on making commercials and guest-starring in shows, among them *Paper Moon* and *Little House on the Prairie*. He also had a nightclub act. His acting career took Hurst by surprise — he had entered college with every intention of becoming a doctor.

Waylon Jennings

Just in case you have trouble following the action on *The Dukes of Hazzard,* there's a friendly balladeer to explain what's going on. Waylon Jennings records his "voice-over" narration after the show is filmed, and the audience doesn't see his face. But Jennings's voice has been familiar since he was one of the youngest disk jockeys in Littlefield, Texas, at the age of twelve. Jennings has since sung backup for the late great Buddy Holly and with the Grateful Dead, and he's become one of the best-selling country recording artists today.

Write to the stars of *The Dukes of Hazzard* at:

The Dukes of Hazzard
℅ Warner Brothers Television
4000 Warner Boulevard
Burbank, CA 91522

DIFF'RENT STROKES (NBC)

Do you remember when the typical American TV family consisted of a mother, a father, and their biological children? That kind of family is rare on television now. In fact, one of the most popular TV families today is about as different from that "typical" model as you can get. That family is the Drummonds, of *Diff'rent Strokes*.

Phillip Drummond was a wealthy white businessman with a fancy Park Avenue apartment. He was a widower and the father of a teenage girl. He employed a black housekeeper, whose own family had never had much money.

When the housekeeper died, Drummond promised he'd look after her orphaned children, Willis and Arnold. Drummond moved the boys into his home — and ultimately adopted them.

That all happened in November 1978, when *Diff'rent Strokes* premiered. Naturally, some adjustments had to be made because people of such different backgrounds were now living under the same roof. But for three years, the Drummonds have been managing to get along with a minimum of trouble and a maximum of fun.

It all goes to show that you don't have to be "typical" to be a success.

Conrad Bain

Conrad Bain keeps his TV family together as Phillip Drummond, father of three energetic and imaginative kids. Bain also had a hand in putting the show together in the first place. He helped come up with the premise (the basic idea of the series), and he helped to pick the other members of the cast.

Bain has experience as a father. He raised three children of his own. He also has experience as an actor — on stage, in films, and on TV. His most visible recent role was as neighbor Arthur Harmon on the series *Maude*.

Gary Coleman

Gary Coleman, as Arnold, plants his feet, tilts his head, squints his eyes, and points his finger. "What you talkin' 'bout?" he demands. The audience breaks into applause and cheers. That's one spunky kid there on the screen.

Gary is a spunky kid off screen, too. He's survived several serious kidney operations. He's traded jokes with Johnny Carson and Lucille Ball on national television. He got his first modeling job by writing to apply for it — at the age of five.

That job led to others, which led to commercials, which led to guest appearances on *America 2-Night, Good Times,* and *The Jeffersons.* When Conrad Bain was talking to his producers about developing *Diff'rent Strokes,* he saw Gary on *The Jeffersons* and thought it would be fun to work with him. Gary has become one of the most recognizable and best-loved kids on television. Last year he won a Youth in Entertainment Award for "Best Young Comedian."

Gary has his own production company, Zephyr Productions. He has starred in the TV movies *The Kid from Left Field* and *Scout's Honor.* He made the feature film *Jimmy the Kid,* and his movie *On the Right Track* was released in 1981. Gary went to work on another TV movie last spring, called *The Littlest Angel.*

Gary's own family is a little more typical than the Drummonds. There's just Gary, his mom, and his dad. The family is separated while Gary works on *Diff'rent Strokes* — his mother stays with him in Hollywood while his father works back home, near Chicago.

Maybe it's the traveling back and forth that makes transportation one of Gary's favorite subjects. He has miles and miles of electric trains in both his homes, and his favorite TV shows are space travel adventures — *Space 1999, Battlestar Galactica,* and *Buck Rogers in the 25th Century.* In fact, one of the best trips Gary ever took was a visit to the 25th century last season — as a guest star in an episode of *Buck Rogers.*

Gary's birthday is February 8. He is thirteen years old.

Todd Bridges

Todd Bridges, who plays Willis, also has a special interest in transportation — last year he built himself a moped. He has also built robots, spaceships, and planes.

Todd comes from a show business family. His mom teaches acting, his dad's an agent, and his older brother and sister are both actors. In fact, Todd's sister is his stand-in on *Diff'rent Strokes*. (She doesn't appear on the show, but goes on the set in his place for things like setting up the lighting for different scenes.) Although he plays the older brother on *Strokes*, Todd is the youngest in his own family. He was also the youngest on his last series, *Fish,* the comedy spin-off from *Barney Miller*.

At sixteen (his birthday is May 27), Todd is a young man of many talents. He is a singer, a dancer, and a fine dramatic actor. He's had roles on *The Waltons, Little House on the Prairie, Police Story, The Love Boat,* and *Here's Boomer*. He made his first record last year.

Dana Plato

Dana Plato has made ninety commercials. She's had parts on the series *Family*, *CHiPs*, and *The Six Million Dollar Man*, and in the ABC Afterschool Special *Schoolboy Father*. She's also appeared in several movies, including *Beyond the Bermuda Triangle* and *California Suite*.

As Kimberly, Dana plays the only Drummond youngster who is biologically related to her father. In real life, Dana was adopted when she was a baby, but her parents separated when she was two. Now seventeen, she lives with her mom.

Dana's birthday is November 7. During time off from the show, she likes to dance, go horseback riding and ice-skating, or listen to music. Her favorite group is Cheap Trick.

You can write to the cast of *Diff'rent Strokes* at:

Diff'rent Strokes
% Tandem Productions
5752 Sunset Boulevard
Los Angeles, CA 90028

THE FACTS OF LIFE
(NBC)

The Facts of Life is a spin-off of *Diff'rent Strokes*. It got its start in the spring of 1980 when the Drummonds' house-keeper, Mrs. Garrett, took a job as housemother in the posh 'n' private Eastland School for Girls. By fall, Mrs. Garrett had been promoted to school dietician, but she remained the adult-in-charge of four of the school's liveliest students.

No one ever goes to class at the Eastland School, and there are few homework assignments or tests. But the girls get a realistic education in values, and they never stop learning about one of the most important facts of life — the meaning of friend-ship.

Charlotte Rae

Charlotte Rae's character, Edna Garrett, must have learned about kids in the same place Abby Bradford (Betty Buckley on *Eight is Enough*) did. She's got the same keep-your-sense-of-humor and discipline-with-love attitude toward her young charges. Maybe it comes from the fact that Charlotte Rae has raised two kids of her own. Or maybe it's because she grew up as a middle child—and she remembers.

Charlotte's talent was discovered by an elementary school

teacher, who helped encourage her to audition for community theater and radio roles. She went on to study drama at Northwestern University with classmates Paul Lynde and Cloris Leachman. Then Charlotte took her act to New York. She wound up on Broadway as Mammy Yokum in *Li'l Abner*.

Charlotte got an Emmy nomination for her TV role in *Queen of the Stardust Ballroom*, and she appeared in the movie version of *Hair*.

Lisa Whelchel

It's hard to make a snobby character likeable, but Lisa Whelchel's wealthy, stuck-up Blair is a delight. It's fun to hate her when she's obnoxious, and it's nice to see how loyal she can really be when her friends are in trouble.

Blair's philosophy is "anything worth doing is worth being patted on the back for" — especially if it's Blair who gets the praise. In real life, Lisa finds a lot of things worth doing. A born-again Christian from Fort Worth, Texas, Lisa is a licensed glider pilot, a singer, a dancer, a guitar player, and a ventriloquist. She also loves skiing, horseback and motorcycle riding, and lots of different sports. She's taken time out from her busy life to get in some movie and TV acting, including parts on *Family*, *The Mary Tyler Moore Show*, and a regular role on *The New Mickey Mouse Club*. She just made the TV movie *Twirl*, with *Happy Days*'s Erin Moran.

Lisa is 18 years old. Her birthday is May 29.

Nancy McKeon

Nancy McKeon was quietly building her own career while her big brother, Philip, played the role of Tommy on the hit series *Alice*. Acting was the goal Nancy had been heading for since she started modeling at the age of two.

Since then she's had parts on *The Love Boat* and the ABC Afterschool Special *Schoolboy Father*, with Dana Plato and

Rob Lowe. Nancy — whose real voice has less of a streetwise quality than she puts on for her *Facts of Life* character, Jo — has also done voices for animated cartoon characters. She spoke for Dolly Dog in *Puppy's Great Adventure* and *Puppy's Amazing Rescue*, Amelia in *The Trouble With Miss Switch*, and Scruffy in *Scruffy*. Last fall, she starred with Patty Duke Astin in *Please Don't Hit Me, Mom*, and she made the TV movie *Starring Peter and Leigh*.

Mindy Cohn

Fifteen-year-old Mindy Cohn had never acted professionally before getting the part of Natalie on *Facts*. She was doing what came naturally — being a student — at the Westlake School in Los Angeles when Charlotte Rae came by to do research for the show. Charlotte felt Mindy would be perfect for the series and arranged to have the role of Natalie created for her.

Mindy says she and Natalie are a lot alike. "I really feel natural playing Natalie," she says. "We have the same sense of humor."

Mindy enjoys acting, but she hasn't decided yet if she wants to do it forever. She hopes to complete her education and

maybe go on to law school.
Mindy's birthday is May 20.

Kim Fields

When Kim Fields auditioned for the part of fun-loving, gossipy Tootie, the show's producers thought she was too short for the role. But they liked her so much that they decided to offer her the job anyway — and to put her on roller skates to give her some height. Kim's grown up since then, so the skates are gone. The big smile and steady stream of wisecracks remain.

Twelve-year-old Kim has been acting for ten years. She was the little girl in the Mrs. Butterworth's commercial, and she's had roles on *Sesame Street* and *Roots: The Next Generations,* and in the movie *The Taking of Pelham 1-2-3.* In 1980, she won the Youth in Entertainment "Best Young Comedienne" Award. Kim's birthday is May 12.

Write to the stars of *The Facts of Life* at:

The Facts of Life
% T.A.T. Communications Co.
5752 Sunset Boulevard
Los Angeles, CA 90028

M*A*S*H (CBS)

How do you make life in a war zone funny? *M*A*S*H* is in its 10th season of doing just that. A spin-off of the popular 1970 movie (which was based on a book by Robert Hooker), the program is set at the front lines of the Korean War, 1950–1952. The characters are the doctors and nurses who staff the 4077th Mobile Army Surgical Hospital. Over the years, these TV characters have become as familiar and well loved as real people.

Of course, the dialogue is witty and bright, and the situations are both funny and heart-tugging. But it's the reality of the people that is the key to *M*A*S*H*'s success. They not only have to cope with the war; they also have to get along with each other! And, as in any real-life situation, that often hinges on keeping your sense of humor.

*M*A*S*H* is a real make-you-feel-good show. After all, the program suggests, if the human spirit is strong enough to triumph in a war zone, just think what we could do back home.

Alan Alda

Alan Alda plays Captain Benjamin Franklin "Hawkeye" Pierce, the wisecracking and able chief surgeon of the 4077th. Alan's been acting since the age of fifteen, when he appeared in summer stock in Barnesville, Pennsylvania. He is the son of actor Robert Alda and the older brother of actor Antony Alda, both of whom have made guest appearances on *M*A*S*H*.

Alan's career has included stage, television, and feature film performances. He was with the improvisational Second City troupe in New York, and he performed in and helped direct the television special *Free to Be . . . You and Me,* which was also released as a record album. He has written and directed — and won several awards for — numerous episodes of *M*A*S*H,* and one season he created another situation comedy called *We'll Get By.* Alan wrote the screenplay for *The Seduction of Joe Tynan,* a movie in which he played a United

States senator; and he wrote, directed, and stars in his latest film, *The Four Seasons*.

Alan is an active supporter of the Equal Rights Amendment and has received honorary doctorates from four colleges. He and his wife, Arlene, a photographer (who also worked on *The Four Seasons*), live in Los Angeles. They have three daughters, Eve, Elizabeth, and Beatrice.

Mike Farrell

Mike Farrell joined *M*A*S*H* in 1975, in the role of Captain B.J. Hunnicutt. B.J. — who has no first name, only the initials — has a much quieter personality, but he has a quick mind and is a good friend to Hawkeye.

Mike grew up in Los Angeles, and his goal was always to be an actor. He has been on stage and in motion pictures, and he had a regular role on the daytime series *Days of Our Lives*. Since joining the cast of *M*A*S*H*, he has appeared in several TV movies, including *Battered* and *Damien, The Leper Priest*. He has also started writing and directing some *M*A*S*H* scripts and he was nominated for a 1980-81 Emmy award for one he co-wrote.

Mike lives in Los Angeles. He has two children, Michael Josh and Erin. (Erin is also the name of B.J.'s daughter on the show.)

Harry Morgan

"Don't go away; we'll be right back," Harry Morgan invites us before the last scene (the "tag") on M*A*S*H. Morgan, who plays Colonel Sherman Potter, commanding officer of the 4077th, has kept coming back for over forty years. One of his most famous roles was as Officer Bill Gannon on the detective series *Dragnet*.

Morgan had every intention of becoming a lawyer while he was growing up; he took up acting as a hobby. He was discovered by a talent scout while performing with a stock company, and offered a contract by 20th Century-Fox. One of his earliest films was *The Oxbow Incident,* a famous movie about frontier justice. Morgan has been in more than fifty films, including *High Noon, Inherit the Wind, Support Your Local Sheriff,* and the Disney film *Snowball Express;* and he's had roles in seven TV series. He appeared as Briggs in last year's TV movie *Scout's Honor,* with Gary Coleman.

Loretta Swit

Loretta Swit's character, Major Margaret Houlihan, has undergone a complete transformation since *M*A*S*H* started in 1972. The most remarkable thing about the change is that it has come about gradually, as though the unit's chief nurse were truly a real person. Margaret has always been a topnotch nurse. But she has changed from a smug, unhappy, power-grasping person into a warm and sensitive woman, much stronger than before. Margaret is a very special TV character — she is capable of learning and of changing because of what she learns.

Loretta was born in New Jersey, and she studied acting in New York. When she moved to Los Angeles in 1969, she made guest appearances on *Gunsmoke* and other top series. *M*A*S*H* gave her her first continuing TV role. She has also been in feature films — did you see her in *Freebie and the Bean?* — and TV movies. Her free-time hobbies include reading (especially about World War II), painting, and romping with her four dogs.

David Ogden Stiers

Stuffy Major Charles Emerson Winchester III is so realistically portrayed by David Ogden Stiers that seeing David in another role is always a shock. The hardest thing to get used to is that David *doesn't* have a Boston accent.

Not that he should — after all, he was born in Peoria, Illinois. But David does have one or two things in common with Charles, especially a love of classical music. He has conducted the orchestra at Lincoln Center in New York, and during the

summer of 1980, he guest-conducted the Portland Symphony Orchestra.

David studied at the Juilliard School in New York, and he has played many dramatic roles on stage. The producers of M*A*S*H discovered him in a guest appearance on the last episode of *The Mary Tyler Moore Show,* and he joined the M*A*S*H cast in 1977. He has been in several TV movies, including *Damien, The Leper Priest,* with Ken *(The White Shadow)* Howard and Mike Farrell, and a CBS Afternoon Playhouse presentation called *Me and Mr. Skinner.*

Jamie Farr

For eight seasons, Corporal Maxwell Q. Klinger wore dresses and high heels in hopes of getting a Section 8 ("psychologically unfit to serve") discharge from the army. But last year when Gary Burghoff — company clerk Radar O'Reilly — left the show, Klinger decided it was worth giving up dresses to take over Radar's job.

Jamie Farr, who plays Klinger, looks as nice in a tuxedo as he does in a skirt. You can see him all spiffed up as a panelist on *The Gong Show* and *The $1.98 Beauty Contest.* He also continues to appear in stage productions and nightclubs during his time off from M*A*S*H, wearing various costumes, depending on the show.

Jamie was in the motion pictures *No Time For Sergeants, The Greatest Story Ever Told,* and *Cannonball Run* with Burt Reynolds. He was recently cast to star in a TV biography of funnyman Jimmy Durante. Jamie and his wife, Joy, live in California with their two children, Jonas and Yvonne.

William Christopher

William Christopher's portrayal of Father Francis Mulcahy, company chaplain, is so convincing it's easy to think he's a real priest. But he isn't. He isn't even the first Father Mulcahy in the role. (Check out the early *M*A*S*H* episodes when they are syndicated in your area.)

William really is like Mulcahy in one way — they are both excellent piano players.

A descendant of Paul Revere, William has pursued his acting career from Evanston, Illinois, to Tamworth, New Hampshire, to New York City, to Los Angeles. His first regular TV role was on *Gomer Pyle, USMC,* and you can catch him in reruns of *Hogan's Heroes, That Girl, The Andy Griffith Show,* and *The Patty Duke Show.* He recently guest-starred on *The Love Boat.*

William and his wife, Barbara — a silk-screen artist and gourmet cook — have two sons, John and Edward.

You can write to the stars of *M*A*S*H* at:

*M*A*S*H*
% 20th Century-Fox Television
P.O. Box 900
Beverly Hills, CA 90213

HAPPY DAYS (ABC)

Happy Days started out as a happy fifteen-minute segment of the old *Love, American Style* show in 1972. The story featured Ron Howard and Anson Williams and was called "Love and the Happy Day." In January 1974, Ron and Anson took starring roles in the situation comedy spin-off. (Ron has since left the show to become a producer of TV movies.)

Happy Days focuses on a group of teenagers growing up in the late 1950s and '60s. It follows the adventures of the super-straight Cunningham family and their friends — one of whom is the super-cool Arthur "Fonzie" Fonzerelli.

Henry Winkler's Fonzie has been so popular that there was once talk of spinning him off into his own show. That idea was shelved because it was said to be the Fonzie–Richie Cunningham (Ron Howard) relationship that made *Happy Days* such a hit. When Ron left the series last year, some of the other character relationships were changed to make them more important. The changes worked, and now, in its second season without Richie, *Happy Days* is still up on top of the ratings.

Henry Winkler

For a while, it made Henry Winkler nervous that people expected him to be "The Fonz" off-screen as well as on. "I am not The Fonz," he wanted to shout. "I am Henry Winkler, and I only wear leather jackets when I work." Then he realized how important his character was to his fans. "We did a show about Fonzie taking out a library card," Henry remembers in an article he wrote for *TV Guide*, "and the American Library Association reported a 500 percent increase in card applications." Henry also realized how much he liked the character. "The Fonz is one of the good guys," he explains in the same article. "He has a strong belief in what's right and what's wrong" — and the courage to act on his convictions.

Henry grew up in New York City, the only child of parents who had emigrated from Germany. Unlike Fonzie, a high school dropout who got his diploma in night school, Henry did well at private school and at Emerson College. He'd decided at the age of seven that he wanted to be an actor, and with that dream still strong, he attended the Yale School of Drama.

Henry had had his first starring role when he was in eighth grade. His first movie, several years later, was *The Lords of Flatbush*, and he has since starred in *The One and Only* and *Heroes*. He played the Scrooge character, Benedict Slade, in the TV movie *An American Christmas Carol*, and he has had his own TV special, *Henry Winkler Meets William Shakespeare*.

Henry has his own production company, Fair Dinkum Productions. ("Fair dinkum" means "honest man"; it comes from the slangy dialect of Australia.) Its first project was the award-winning *Who Are the DeBolts . . . And Why Do They Have 19 Kids?* in 1979.

Fonzie's first leather jacket — like Archie Bunker's original living room chair — is on display at the Smithsonian Institution, in Washington, D.C. "It means that *Happy Days* has created history," Henry says proudly. He and his wife, Stacey Weitzman, live with their two children in California.

Tom Bosley

The name "Bosley" may conjure up two images in your mind — David Doyle's character on *Charlie's Angels* and Howard Cunningham on *Happy Days*. In fact, the Angels' guardian was named for Tom Bosley, an award-winning performer for over thirty years.

Tom Bosley's first smash success was on Broadway, playing the title role in the 1959 musical *Fiorello!* (The show was a biography of Fiorello La Guardia, one of the most colorful mayors in New York City history.) Tom broke show business records in the role by becoming the first actor to win all four major theater awards in the same season (the Tony, Drama Critics, ANTA, and Newspaper Guild awards).

Tom's been appearing in movies since 1962, and he's had continuing roles or guest appearances in more than five hundred television shows. His voice is featured on the animated Christmas special *The Stingiest Man in Town*. Tom's latest continuing role — at the same time as *Happy Days* — is as the new man from Glad.

Marion Ross

In addition to playing mama Cunningham, Marion Ross has been in the motion pictures *Operation Petticoat, Airport,* and *Grand Theft Auto* — the last with Ron Howard. During the 1980–81 season, she appeared in the TV movie *Skyward,* which Howard produced. She has had roles on *The Untouchables, Perry Mason, Marcus Welby, M.D., Hawaii Five-O,* and *The Love Boat;* and she starred with *Little House on the Prairie*'s Melissa Sue Anderson in the ABC Afterschool Special *Which Mother is Mine?*

Erin Moran

When *Happy Days* started, Erin Moran's Joanie Cunningham was a pesky little sister. She has since grown up to be a cheerful, well-adjusted high school graduate who just

happens to have something going with the handsome Chachi, played by Scott Baio.

Erin started acting in commercials when she was six years old. She's done guest appearances on *Gunsmoke*, *The FBI*, *The Courtship of Eddie's Father*, *My Three Sons*, *Family Affair*, *The Waltons*, and *The Love Boat;* and she appeared with Anson Williams in the Hallmark Hall of Fame production *Lisa, Bright and Dark*.

Erin's birthday is October 18. She has five brothers and sisters, and the family owns a dog, five cats, and three horses.

Scott Baio

You can't open your favorite fan magazine without seeing a story on Scott Baio — but would you want to? This young man would tie with John "Bo Duke" Schneider in a contest for TV's "Most Popular Fellow."

Scott has been playing Chachi Arcola, Fonzie's drum-playing cousin, since 1977. And he's been Joanie Cunningham's favorite guy since last season, when high school romance bloomed.

Scott's career started when he was ten years old. He had modeling jobs at first, then moved to doing commercials. His first big role was the title part in *Bugsy Malone*, with Jodie Foster. That's since been followed by *Foxes* and *Skatetown, USA*. Aside from *Happy Days*, Scott's had TV roles on *Blansky's Beauties*, *Who's Watching the Kids?*, *Good Time Girls*, and *Here's Boomer*. He also starred in the ABC Afterschool specials *The Boy Who Drank Too Much*, *Luke Was There*, and last season's *Stoned* and *Run, Don't Walk*. (That one, by the way, was produced by Henry Winkler's Fair Dinkum Productions.)

Scott's role in *Run, Don't Walk* was that of a high school student confined to a wheelchair. He helps a girl in his class come to terms with *her* new wheelchair. A natural athlete who has participated in several TV celebrity challenges, Scott took up body-building to prepare for the role. (A person using a manually operated wheelchair has well-developed muscles in the upper part of his body.) He liked it so much that he's kept up the weight-lifting — along with basketball, football, baseball, and racquetball.

Over last summer, Scott made the feature film *The Wiz Kid* and the TV movie *Senior Trip*. He also began hosting the syndicated TV series *We're Movin'*.

Scott, who was born on September 22, is the youngest of three children. Steve and Stephanie are twins, and Steve has launched his own acting career with small roles in the movies *Saturday Night Fever* and *An Unmarried Woman*.

During his scarce free time, Scott likes to listen to music. His favorite singer is Billy Joel.

Anson Williams

Don't let Potsie Webber's lazy grin fool you. The man behind that smile is talented in several fields — *and* he's a smart businessman. You can see evidence of some of that right on the show. With his partner, Ron Rose, Anson Williams writes the songs that he performs on *Happy Days*. He is also a scriptwriter and a producer, and he put both of those skills to work last fall on the TV movie *Skyward*.

Anson is married to actress Lorrie Mahaffey, who played his girlfriend on several episodes of the series. (She also co-starred with Scott Baio and Lynda Goodfriend on the short-lived series *Who's Watching the Kids?*)

In his time off from *Happy Days*, Anson is as likely to be singing or emceeing a charity benefit as he is to be appearing on a game or talk show. He and Ron Rose wrote the American Heart Association's theme song for 1980. His first commercial hit song was "Deeply," released in 1977.

Al Molinaro

Al Molinaro (Al Delvecchio) got his first acting role by mistake, when the casting director of *Green Acres* mixed him up with someone else. But he did so well that he got the role of Agent 44 on the *Get Smart* series. Al met *Happy Days* producer Garry Marshall when Marshall was looking for someone to play Murray the Cop on *The Odd Couple* series. Al had the part for five years. Since taking over Arnold's — now known as Fonzie's and Al's — Molinaro has also appeared on *Fantasy Island* and the TV special *With Anson and Lorrie*.

Lynda Goodfriend

Lynda Goodfriend has become good friends with the other members of the *Happy Days* cast by acting in several different shows with them. Originally trained to be a dancer, Lynda's first TV role was a guest shot on the series. She played Richie's girlfriend, Lori Beth Allen, in several different episodes. Ironically, her role became permanent *after* Ron Howard left the show. Now Lori Beth's a waitress at Fonzie's and Al's.

In between, Lynda had roles on *Blansky's Beauties* (with Scott Baio) and on *Who's Watching the Kids?* (with Scott and with Lorrie Mahaffey, Anson Williams' wife).

Lynda was a baton twirler and string bass player in high school — where she also achieved straight A's. She likes mountain climbing and photography, and she is a licensed pilot. Her birthday is on Halloween.

Cathy Silvers

"Jenny Piccalo is loud, open, honest, and a troublemaker," Cathy Silvers says of her character. Cathy left out one important trait — last year Jenny became *visible*. Although she's always been important to the show as Joanie's boy-crazy best friend, Jenny was someone the audience often heard about but never saw.

Cathy herself has been visible to audiences ever since she could walk. Her first appearance was on stage at a Las Vegas hotel where her father, entertainer Phil Silvers, was doing his act. *Happy Days* is her first professional assignment, although she had parts in stage plays throughout high school and college. She sharpened her vocal and verbal skills on the debating team.

Cathy has four sisters (one of them, Candy, is also her twin). She is a gymnast and sports enthusiast, but she likes quieter activities, too, such as reading and going to the movies.

Ted McGinley

There was one too few Cunninghams around the house when Richie left. Enter history teacher/basketball coach Roger Phillips, a relative of Marion Cunningham. Ted McGinley, who plays the role, was discovered the same way Ralph Macchio (of *Eight is Enough*) was — during an ABC talent search.

Ted had a role in the 1979 TV movie *Valentine*, with Jack Albertson.

Write to the cast of *Happy Days* at:

Happy Days
℅ Paramount Television
5451 Marathon Street
Los Angeles, CA 90038

LAVERNE & SHIRLEY (ABC)

Shirley Feeney and Laverne DeFazio lead extraordinary lives. In fact, in more than five seasons, not one single normal thing has ever happened to them! They can't do a good deed without getting stranded on a rooftop, they can't live in California without going through a major earthquake — they can't even get through an earthquake without swinging from the chandelier.

That kind of life may sound tiring, but Laverne and Shirley seem used to it — they come back every week for more, as full of energy and good spirits as ever.

Shirley and Laverne started out as friends of Fonzie in an episode of *Happy Days*. With their working-class background, blue collar jobs, and lack of much formal education, they seem to have something in common with Archie Bunker, too — though their personalities are usually more pleasant.

Last year, the girls left Milwaukee and their jobs there in the Shotz Brewery, to move to sunny — and earthquake-y — Los Angeles. Life hasn't changed much for them, though — everyone they know moved, too!

Penny Marshall

The characters on a situation comedy often behave like family members toward each other, even if they're not related. This happens on *Laverne & Shirley*, where, for instance, Lenny and Squiggy are almost like brothers, to each other and to the

girls. There's a *real* family involved in the show, too. Penny Marshall, who stars as Laverne, works in front of the camera. Behind the scenes are producer Tony Marshall, her father; and executive producer Garry Marshall, her brother. Her sister Ronny Hallin, is the producer of *Happy Days*.

On the show, Penny plays a young woman barely out of her teens. In real life, she is the mother of a teenage daughter, Tracy. Penny has had parts on several TV series, and you can still catch her in the role of Myrna Turner on reruns of *The Odd Couple*.

Penny has tried her hand at directing TV episodes, too, and she likes it. "You don't have to worry about how you look" when you're *behind* a camera, she says. She can often be found with a glass of her favorite drink — milk and Pepsi — close by, just like Laverne.

Cindy Williams

Cindy Williams turned down the role of Shirley Feeney the first several times it was offered to her; there were other things she wanted to be doing. She was planning to be in a play, and she had dreams of becoming a movie star. Garry Marshall finally convinced her to give it a try, and Cindy found she liked the character and the early '60s setting. She's played characters from the same time period in some of her subsequent films, including *American Graffiti* and *More American Graffiti*.

Cindy shares Shirley's love for animals, especially cats, and she is National Chairwoman of the Fund for Animals. About ten years older than Shirley in real life, Cindy is single and has an older brother and a younger sister.

David L. Lander and Michael McKean

Just as it's hard to talk about Lenny without mentioning Squiggy, it's hard to mention Michael McKean without talking about David L. Lander. The actors have been a team since before *Laverne & Shirley* was conceived.

Squiggy and Lenny came into being at Carnegie-Mellon University, in Pittsburgh, where David and Michael met while studying acting. The actors and their characters moved out to Hollywood and continued to work together often, touring the country with a satirical comedy group called The Credibility Gap. David and Michael had separate guest appearances on various TV shows and came together to perform as Lenny and the Squiggtones, an act that's been recorded as an album.

David and Michael both live in the Los Angeles area — David with his wife, Kathy; and Michael with his wife, Susan, and their son, Colin.

Phil Foster

Sometimes when you're standing in line waiting to get into a movie, street performers will appear to entertain you with juggling acts, singing, or instrument playing. Phil Foster, who plays Laverne's father, Frank, started his show business career singing and dancing outside of movie theaters over forty years ago. He soon moved inside to appear in amateur shows, where he could compete for prizes. He's since won opportunities to perform in every English-speaking country in the world.

In addition to acting, Foster is a scriptwriter and a teacher. He runs a comedy school in Los Angeles called the Foster Children. The only fee for taking his classes is a pledge to help other aspiring actors when a graduate gets the chance.

Betty Garrett

Nobody does just *one* thing. Betty Garrett's character, Edna, is no exception. She started out as Laverne and Shirley's landlady in Milwaukee, and soon became Laverne's stepmother as well. Now Edna helps her husband, Frank, run his Los Angeles eatery.

Betty Garrett can do more than one thing, too. In addition

to acting, she dances and sings. She's done Hollywood films, Broadway musicals, straight stage plays, and nightclub acts.

Betty had two seasons as Archie Bunker's neighbor, Irene, before coming to *Laverne & Shirley*.

Eddie Mekka

Gymnastics and opera. That's some combination. But it's *the* combination that brought Eddie Mekka to his role as Carmine Ragusa on *Laverne & Shirley*.

Eddie, born Edward Rudolph Mekjian (the name is Armenian), expected to become a gym teacher. He'd had training in voice, but performing in opera wasn't quite what he wanted to spend his whole life doing. Then he attended a local theater production of *Hello, Dolly!* The actors seemed to be having so much fun. "I could do that," Eddie thought, and he went backstage to ask for a job. He wasn't hired but he decided to take advantage of his gymnastics training, as a springboard to learning to dance, and soon Eddie had a role in a touring company of *Promises, Promises*. Encouraged, he headed for Broadway, where he appeared in *Lieutenant: A Rock Opera,* a musical about Lt. Calley and the My Lai massacre in Vietnam. The show closed after a week, but Eddie won a Tony Award nomination for his performance.

Next stop — Hollywood, where he got the part of "The Great Ragoo" in short order.

Eddie continues his singing and dancing both as Carmine and in his time off from the show. Single, he has older twin brothers and one sister, and he lives in California.

Write to the cast of *Laverne & Shirley* at:

Laverne & Shirley
% Paramount Television
5451 Marathon Street
Los Angeles, CA 90038

THE LOVE BOAT
(ABC)

What well-traveled ship has managed to stay "exciting and new" for more than four seasons? *The Love Boat*! The magic isn't in the *SS Pacific Princess's* paint job. It's another formula that keeps this luxury ship merrily afloat: lots of romance and lots of guest stars.

Every week, three lucky couples on the Los Angeles-to-Mexico-and-back cruise overcome all obstacles and find eternal happiness by falling in love. Realistic? Hardly. Fun? You bet!

The passenger list changes weekly, of course. But *The Love Boat* has its own permanent crew of stars. Come aboard and meet them.

Gavin MacLeod

Gavin MacLeod has made almost forty films and appeared in more than three hundred fifty television series. His most famous roles before *The Love Boat*'s Captain Merrill Stubing were Happy on *McHale's Navy* and newswriter Murray Slaughter on *The Mary Tyler Moore Show*.

Fred Grandy

Fred Grandy's character, yeoman-purser Burl ''Gopher'' Smith, is a well-meaning, cheerful young man who often takes the long way to get to the right answer. In real life, Fred spent some time as a speechwriter for a U.S. congressman before he decided that he wanted to be an actor.

That must have been the right decision, because he was soon

named the Best Supporting Actor of the 1972–73 off-Broadway season, in New York.

Before *The Love Boat* became a series, it appeared as three TV movies (based, by the way, on Jeraldine Saunders's book, *The Love Boats*). Fred has played Gopher since the beginning. He now also writes scripts for some of the episodes, either alone or with Bernie Kopell.

Bernie Kopell

Bernie Kopell, "Doc" Adam Bricker, was discovered in a taxicab — while he was driving it. It seems that one day he was taking a producer to the airport. You know how one thing leads to another. Well, this trip led to Bernie's first movie role.

Soon Bernie was working steadily on television. He played Siegfried on *Get Smart* and Jerry on *That Girl*. He had four different parts in various episodes of *Bewitched*.

Now Bernie is adding writing credits to his acting ones. He's already co-authored several *Love Boat* segments with co-star Fred Grandy.

Ted Lange

"The best bartenders are both great listeners and great entertainers," Ted Lange says. "Watch how they work with their hands." Ted studied bartenders and bartending to prepare for his role as *The Love Boat*'s Isaac Washington. "I had to," he says. "I wanted to do it right."

In addition to acting, Ted directs and writes. He has a wide range — he's directed a production of Neil Simon's *The Odd Couple*, several Shakespearean plays, and two films. He has also served as Honorary Mayor of Reseda (a suburb of Los Angeles), California, where he lives with his wife, Sherryl, and their son, Ted IV.

Lauren Tewes

The job of a cruise director — like Lauren Tewes's character, Julie McCoy — is to bring people together and make sure they're having fun. Lauren got into show business in order to get together with people. She started auditioning for community theater roles when she was eleven, hoping to make friends.

Lauren has been in many commercials — she once had twenty on the air at the same time. She had a role in the TV movie *The Dallas Cowboy Cheerleaders,* and she's been with *The Love Boat* since the third TV movie/pilot.

Jill Whelan

Jill Whelan's first big career decision was whether to join a national touring company as one of the orphans in *Annie* or to audition for a TV series. She chose TV and eventually wound up as Vicki Stubing, the Captain's daughter. Jill has also appeared on *Fantasy Island* and in the feature film *Airplane*.

Jill's interests — aside from a passion for *Gone with the Wind,* and her doll collection — are mostly musical. She sings, dances, and plays the piano.

You can write to the crew of *The Love Boat* at:

The Love Boat
% Aaron Spelling Productions
10201 West Pico Boulevard
Los Angeles, CA 90035

CHiPs (NBC)

If you had to put *CHiPs* into one of the standard television programming categories, which one would you choose?

Although the series has elements of comedy and drama, its main ingredients are cycle chases and excitement. But before you classify *CHiPs* as action/adventure, consider this: *CHiPs* could be thought of as a modern-day Western.

Sure, the horses have been traded in for horsepower, and the bad guys hustle along in gas guzzlers instead of rustling those little dogies (cattle). But California Highway Patrollers Frank Poncherello and Jon Baker wear the badges of the good guys, and they ride out regularly to protect their territory from (urban) outlaws.

So, you decide. Action/adventure or new-fashioned Western? Either way, Ponch and Jon are back in the saddle each week with a new episode of *CHiPs*.

Erik Estrada

While playing the role of Ponch, Erik Estrada has had two serious motorcycle accidents. One was during the summer of 1979, the other was last spring, while Erik was working on the pilot of a spin-off from *CHiPs* (about two female CHiPs officers).

Erik is no stranger to trouble. He grew up in the tough streets of New York's Spanish Harlem. His Puerto Rican parents were divorced when he was two, and his mom worked hard to keep her family together (Erik has a brother and a sister). When he was just thirteen, Erik had the shock of discovering the body

of his best friend, who died of a drug overdose.

Erik's mother hoped he would grow up to be a policeman, but Erik wanted to act from the time he was in high school. "Poor kids learn they have to work for what they want," Erik says, and he did just that, taking jobs as a waiter and putting aside plans for marrying and having a family until he could get established.

CHiPs is now in its fifth season, with early episodes already in reruns in some parts of the country. Erik loves doing the show and he hopes to *keep* doing it, but he is already looking ahead. He's got plans to do two TV movies each year, and at least two feature films are set. One is *Body and Soul,* about a boxer (a remake of a movie that starred John Garfield). The other is *The Cisco Kid,* a comic Western.

Erik is pleased with his success and proud of his role as Officer Poncherello. "I like to think of myself as the Great Brown Hope," he says, "a positive Hispanic role model."

Larry Wilcox

Officer Jon Baker may be a laid-back 'n' mellow, quiet kind of guy, but on his own time Larry Wilcox is always in the thick of the action. A Vietnam war veteran, Larry is a champion steer-roper who alternates weekends riding in rodeos and riding in dirt bike competitions. He's won events in both and often does his own stunts on *CHiPs.* Larry also raises thoroughbred horses on his thirty-acre ranch, sings, plays the guitar, and is moving from acting to directing and producing. He has his own production company, Flying Diamond Enterprises, named for the family ranch (since sold) where he grew up. One of the company's projects is a film called *Tell the World We're Here,* about M.I.A.'s in Vietnam.

Larry's early plan was to become a dentist. He was financing his education by acting in commercials when he realized he wanted to make acting a full-time career. During his two years in the cast of *Lassie,* he became interested in directing and has

directed several episodes of *CHiPs*.

Larry has two children, Derek and Heidi, from his first marriage. In April 1980, he married Hannie Strasser, a member (now a former member) of the sound crew on *CHiPs*. They have a baby daughter, Wendy.

Robert Pine

Larry Wilcox planned to be a dentist. Robert Pine went to medical school. Like his co-worker, Pine found out he'd rather perform on televison than in an operating theater. He wound up as Sergeant Joe Getraer, Ponch and Jon's boss on *CHiPs*.

Pine has been in several Walt Disney movies and has had guest roles on *Charlie's Angels, Medical Center, Doc,* and *The Bob Newhart Show*. He is married to actress Gwynne Gilford, and their daughter, Katie, is nine years old.

Randi Oakes

Randi Oakes started out as a bad guy on *CHiPs,* in a guest-starring role as a car thief. She did so well, she was offered the continuing role of Officer Bonnie Clark.

In just one day of working on *CHiPS,* Randi sees more people than she ran into during the first sixteen years of her life. She grew up in a small Iowa town with a population of fifty, and there were only fifty students in her class at the regional high school.

After winning a modeling contest, Randi moved to New York to start her first career. As a top model, she traveled all over the world for seven years. She was taking acting lessons at the same time and finally decided it was time to settle in Los Angeles for career No. 2: acting. Guest appearances on several series and TV movies brought her to *CHiPs,* where she's been riding happily ever since.

Bruce Jenner

Olympic champion Bruce Jenner signed on as a recurring *CHiPs* character last fall: motorcycle patrolman Steve Mc-Leish. Bruce has spent lots of time on TV in the last few years. Since he won the Gold Medal in 1976 for his record-breaking achievements in the Decathlon, he has appeared as a network sportscaster and interviewer, and as the spokesperson in several commercials. (Who could better promote the "breakfast of champions"?) Last summer he hosted *Summer Season,* NBC's replacement-during-the-strike for Saturday afternoon baseball.

In addition to being a track and TV star, Bruce is also an author. He co-wrote *Decathlon Challenge: Bruce Jenner's Story* with Phillip Finch (Prentice-Hall, 1977), *Bruce Jenner's Guide to the Olympics* with Marc Abraham (Andrews & McMeel, 1979), and *The Olympics and Me* with R. Smith Kiliper (Doubleday, 1980).

You can write to the stars of *CHiPs* at:

CHiPs
℅ MGM Television
10202 West Washington Boulevard
Culver City, CA 90230

GENERAL HOSPITAL's Luke and Laura

Romance. Mystery. Crime. Suspense. Excitement. Some good times, and a lot of bad times. You expect all of these things in a daytime drama — and you find them on *General Hospital* (ABC). You find something more, too — a sense of humor

Luke Spencer, for example, spends more time *in* trouble than *out* of it. But he never lets trouble get him down. He's always got another plan. And when his plans fall apart, he's as quick to come up with an excuse as if he were a student who forgot his homework.

Laura Baldwin, the love of Luke's life, keeps her sense of humor, too. For her it's self-defense. If you took a devil-may-care guy like Luke too seriously, you'd *really* be in trouble!

Luke and Laura did not meet under the best of circumstances. In fact, Laura hated Luke at first, and soon after meeting him she married someone else. But then Luke got into some serious trouble — he knew too much about a huge, stolen stash of gold — and Laura discovered that she cared about him. Luke and Laura spent a summer on the run, falling in love all along the way.

The course of true love never does run smoothly. That special summer was a year and a half ago, and Luke and Laura still have problems. How will things work out? Tune in tomorrow . . .

Anthony Geary

Handsome Luke Spencer is played by handsome Anthony Geary — who doesn't really look like Luke! "I had my hair lightened and permed for the part," Tony says. "I may look totally different in my next role."

Tony grew up in the tiny mining town of Coalville, Utah. He always knew he'd rather be up on a stage than down in a mine, so he studied drama at the University of Utah. Named a Presidential Award Scholar in theater, Tony got his first professional role while he was still in school. Actor Jack Albertson (*Chico and the Man, Valentine*) came to a school performance and offered Tony a part in the play Albertson was taking on the road.

Tony had parts in more than forty plays around the country before he went to Los Angeles to be in the film *Johnny Got His Gun*. That's when he found out that performing on screen could be as much fun as performing on stage. Tony settled in L.A. He had guest parts in many top TV shows, including *Mannix, The Mod Squad, Room 222, Barnaby Jones, The Streets of San Francisco, All in the Family,* and *The Blue Knight*. He was so good that he was invited back to some of these shows several times.

Tony had roles on the daytime dramas *Bright Promise* and *The Young and the Restless* before joining *General Hospital* in the summer of 1980. He had also produced an award-winning children's story for public radio, called *Sound of Sunshine, Sound of Rain*. He liked doing that so much that eventually he would like to produce and direct full-time.

You might get the feeling that Tony has a good time *whatever* he's doing. That's as true off camera as on. In his free time Tony likes to keep himself in lean, lanky shape by scuba diving, surfing, horseback riding, roller skating, and dancing. Sometimes, too, Tony just likes to get away from it all. He'll hop on a plane, all by himself, and go somewhere new — often to a foreign country.

Single, Tony lives in Los Angeles and has two sisters, Deann and Jana. His birthday is May 29.

Genie Francis

Laura Baldwin has been through enough problems to have lived several lifetimes. She committed a murder. She was the victim of an assault. She's been married and separated. Daughter of a doctor, she's been involved with crime and underworld heavies. Genie Francis, the actress who's taken Laura through all these adventures, is only nineteen years old. "Doing the role has speeded up my growth process," Genie says.

Genie's been playing Laura since she was fourteen. It was her second professional acting job, following a guest appearance on *Family*.

Both Genie's parents are actors, and she decided early that she wanted to get into the profession, too. She choreographed, directed, and starred in her first stage play when she was twelve. "I loved the applause," Genie says. A career was begun.

Genie's high school graduation was celebrated on the set of *General Hospital*. She attends college on a part-time basis and hopes eventually to move from television to films. She's already gotten a start in TV movies, with a role in last season's *Oklahoma City Dolls*.

Genie's birthday is May 26. She has two brothers and lives in Los Angeles with her parents.

You can write to the stars of *General Hospital* at:

General Hospital
% ABC-TV
4151 Prospect Avenue
Hollywood, CA 90027

LITTLE HOUSE's
Matt and Pat

Little House on the Prairie (NBC) is set in the American Midwest at the turn of the century. It's based on the nine books that Laura Ingalls Wilder wrote about her own growing-up years.

Little House is a family show in several senses of the word. It's a show you can *watch* with your whole family. It's a show *about* families. And it's a show that *stars* families.

Melissa Gilbert, who plays Laura, is the real-life sister of Jonathan Gilbert, who plays Willie Oleson. Twins Lindsay and Sidney Greenbush share the role of Laura's sister, Carrie; and the littlest Ingalls sister, Grace, is played by Wendi and Brenda Turnbaugh. (Young children are allowed to work only a few hours a day in TV or movies, so their parts are often shared by identical twins.) And **Matthew Laborteaux,** who plays the Ingalls's adopted son, Albert, is the real-life brother of **Patrick Laborteaux,** who plays Andy Garvey.

Pat and Matt Laborteaux were adopted by their parents when they were babies. They are not biologically related, but they are "real" brothers — and part of a real family — in every other way. About a year apart in age, they are also very close friends. (Pat was sixteen on July 22; Matt was fifteen on December 8.)

Pat started acting when he was three and a half years old. Matt got into the business at age four, when a director found out that Matt could cry on cue. That was a particularly special talent since Matt didn't start *talking* until he was five. (It was

lucky that he didn't have much dialogue to learn for his first movie, *Woman Under the Influence*.)

Pat and Matt appeared on stage together for the first time when Pat was eight and Matt was seven. Pat was already pursuing other interests besides acting — especially swimming (at which he is now a champion), drawing, and bowling. Pat has a collection of two thousand comic books and hopes someday to publish his *own* comic books (he'll create his own characters and write the stories, too). In the meantime, his role on *Little House* leaves him enough free time to audition for other shows. He had a guest part on *Aloha Paradise* when that show started last spring.

Matt first worked on *Little House* when he was cast as young Charles Ingalls for a flashback in a single episode. He got the steady role of Albert two years later. Matt appeared in the NBC Special Treat *Papa and Me,* about a boy and his dying grandfather, and he was host of a TV special last season called *True Legends of the West.* Matt sticks to a special diet to correct for low blood sugar (the same problem Burt Reynolds has), and he loves classical music.

Both Pat and Matt do work for the Youth Rescue Fund, an organization that raises money to help the National Network for Runaways and Youth Services.

You can write to *any* of the actors on *Little House* at:

Little House on the Prairie
% MGM Television
10202 West Washington Boulevard
Culver City, CA 90230

THREE'S COMPANY

(ABC)

When Janet Wood and Chrissy Snow lost their roommate at the start of this series, they needed a replacement to help pay the rent. Somehow none of the young women they interviewed clicked. Then along came Jack Tripper. He was a nice guy, he really needed a place to stay, and he was a fabulous cook. What more could you want? Janet insisted that the relationship be "just friends," and Jack agreed. He moved in.

Janet, Jack, and Chrissy got along fine for more than five seasons. Jack couldn't always stick to the agreement, but the women helped him out when he slipped. When Chrissy (Suzanne Somers) left the apartment and the show last spring, her cousin Cindy moved in. She's been replaced as a roommate by Terri, a nurse (though Cindy is still a character on the show), and the new threesome gets along fine, too.

In fact, this program could be called *Very Good Friends*. Because, really, that's what Jack, Janet, and Terri are. Every week they get themselves into impossible situations that prove two points: (1) it takes work to be very good friends with someone of the opposite sex in particular — and roommates in general — and (2) it's worth the effort.

Three's Company is a success mostly because it's silly good fun. But it also fulfills the very nice fantasy that males and females *can* get along — even when they have to live together.

John Ritter

Whether he's doing comedy or drama, there's something about John Ritter that inspires confidence. He looks like the kind of person you'd like to put your arms around and give all your trust. It's a quality that made him believable as the slightly zany Captain Avenger in the 1980 film *Hero at Large*. It also made him a perfect choice for the recurring role of Reverend Fordwick on *The Waltons*. And it's there in his portrayal of Jack Tripper.

John comes from a show business family. His dad was Tex Ritter, a movie cowboy and country-and-western singer, who died in 1974. His mom, Dorothy Fay, had a career as an actress. John's older brother, Thomas, is a lawyer, and for a long time John considered going into politics. But, he says, "I was never sure *what* I wanted to be." His parents guessed the direction John would take when he made his first movie, with friends, at the age of twelve. And John finally figured it out himself after spending two summers traveling and performing in Europe with his college acting troupe. "That solidified things for me," John says.

He returned to the States and played serious roles in such plays as *The Glass Menagerie* and *Butterflies Are Free*. He also worked on developing his comic abilities, and during this time he met and became close friends with TV's Mork, Robin Williams.

John has had guest appearances on *M*A*S*H*, *Kojak*, *Hawaii Five-O*, *The Bob Newhart Show*, *Medical Center*, *Phyllis*, *Rhoda*, and *Starsky and Hutch;* and he's starred in the TV movies *Leave Yesterday Behind* and *The Comeback Kid*. With his wife, Nancy Morgan, he appeared in *Americathon*, a futuristic movie set in 1998, and last spring he completed filming on the motion picture *They All Laughed*. He also just starred in the TV movie *Pray TV*.

John enjoys all kinds of sports, listening to Beatles music, and, with Nancy, raising their son, Jason.

Joyce DeWitt

Growing up in West Virginia and Indiana, Joyce DeWitt got some real-life training for her role as Janet Wood. She had plenty of "roommates" — a brother and two sisters. And if Janet often finds herself caught between her *Three's Company* roomies, Joyce knows about that, too, having been the middle sister.

Joyce always wanted to act, but her father wanted her to find a more sensible career. So she double-majored at Ball State University in Indiana, earning a theater degree and teacher credentials. She also developed her talents for singing and dancing, but still had to spend a long time working as a secretary before getting her first TV role. It was a guest shot on *Baretta*, and it was followed by appearances on other TV series and a part in the TV movie *With This Ring*.

Joyce lives near the beach in sunny Southern California, and she likes to jog, do yoga, meditate, and sail. She's keeping up with her music and singing, and she goes to the movies every chance she gets.

Jenilee Harrison

When Chrissy had to go home to take care of her ailing mother — leaving her roomates short one-third of the rent money — Jenilee Harrison showed up to save the day. As Cindy Snow, Chrissy's cousin, she moved into Jack's and Janet's apartment temporarily. Cindy moved out of the apartment last fall, but she's still on the show. Now she lives at college, where she's studying veterinary medicine.

Jenilee got into television by way of the Los Angeles Rams. As a cheerleader for the pro football team, she was invited to appear on TV variety specials and in ABC's *Battle of the Network Stars* and *Celebrity Challenge of the Sexes*.

Her acting training included modeling, community theater, and studying with a troupe that may sound familiar — the James Best Theater Group. (Yes, that's the same James Best who is now *The Dukes of Hazzard*'s Sheriff Roscoe P. Coltrane.)

Jenilee started this fall season with a bang, starring in the season opener of *The Love Boat*.

Don Knotts

"The happiest days of my life were on *The Andy Griffith Show*," Don Knotts says. From 1960 to 1965 (the show continued until 1968), he played the bumbling deputy Barney Fife — and won five Emmy Awards. But you only have to watch Knotts play landlord Ralph Furley on *Three's Company* to know he's still having a good time.

Knotts has starred in almost twenty feature films, many of which were made for Walt Disney Productions. He's been in *It's A Mad, Mad, Mad, Mad World, The Shakiest Gun in the West, Herbie Goes to Monte Carlo, The Apple Dumpling Gang,* and *The Apple Dumpling Gang Rides Again. The Private Eyes,* co-starring Tim Conway, was released last fall. He's also had regular roles on several TV shows, including *The Don Knotts Show*.

Knotts and his wife, Loralee, have two grown children, Tom and Karen.

Priscilla Barnes

Priscilla Barnes joined the cast of *Three's Company* last fall as Jack and Janet's new roommate. Priscilla plays Terri, a registered nurse who works in a hospital emergency ward.

Living in a new place is something Priscilla knows a lot about. Her father's Air Force career meant frequent moves for the Barnes family while Priscilla was growing up.

Priscilla's career in the public eye began when she started entering beauty pageants. She won several titles and was second runner-up in the Miss California pageant.

Priscilla sings and dances, and she's had roles in TV series,

TV movies, and feature films. She starred in *The American Girls,* a 1978 TV show. Today, when she isn't performing or taking acting classes, Priscilla enjoys collecting artwork for her gallery in Beverly Hills, California.

Richard Kline

Richard Kline's character, Larry, sometimes suspects he's doing something wrong. How come Jack Tripper has all the luck, living with Janet and Terri?

Well, Richard has nothing to be ashamed of. His TV credits include many commercials, as well as roles on *Fernwood 2-night, The Mary Tyler Moore Show, Maude, The Ropers,* and *The Love Boat.* He was also in the TV mini-series *Seventh Avenue.*

On the serious side, too, are his stage credentials, earned after a three-year stint in the army. Richard has played Harry Houdini and Henry V, and he's done *Death of a Salesman, Come Blow Your Horn,* and *The Sunshine Boys.*

Richard and his wife, actress Kathleen Doyle (she appeared in *Roots: The Next Generations*) have two cats and a dog. When Richard isn't busy taping *Three's Company* or playing tennis or cards, he's pursuing a second career as a scriptwriter.

Write to the stars of *Three's Company* at:

Three's Company
% The NRW Company
7800 Beverly Boulevard
Los Angeles, CA 90036

THE POWERS OF
Peter Barton

Who ever said that growing up is easy? Not anyone who's been through it, that's for sure. Part of being a teenager is trying to figure out who you are and where you're going — and what talents you've got that will get you there. It's a serious business that can sometimes leave you feeling out of control.

Well, if things have started being that way for you, you can sympathize with the title character in *The Powers of Matthew Star* (NBC). Matthew seems like an ordinary — though very good-looking — teenager. But when he goes out of control, look out. When Matthew turned fifteen, he developed some special — and confusing — talents. He found he could move things with his mind, read other people's minds, and tell the future. Sometimes.

We learn, before Matthew does, that he was actually born on a distant planet and brought to Earth as an infant. Someday he will return home to be a hero. In the meantime, Matthew is just trying his best to be a normal American kid.

Peter Barton, who plays Matthew, was in his third year of studying to be a pharmacist when he decided to switch to modeling and acting. His family and friends had been telling him for years that his handsome face ought to be in pictures. He finally had some snapshots taken and visited an agent. He started modeling almost at once, and he began taking acting lessons at the same time.

Peter had had only a tiny one-day role on *All My Children* when he auditioned for and won the part of Bill Miller on the series *Shirley*.

Peter was born and grew up on Long Island. He now lives in Los Angeles. Peter is unmarried, and his birthday is July 19.

You can write to Peter at:

> *The Powers of Matthew Star*
> ℅ Paramount Television
> 5451 Marathon Street
> Los Angeles, CA 90038

HILL STREET BLUES's Hill, Renko, and Belker

What is the closest personal relationship that exists in the world? Between a mother and her child? Between a husband and wife? If you watch *Hill Street Blues* (NBC), another possible answer will come to your mind: There is no one closer than a policeman and his partner. A cop's life can depend every day on the trustworthiness of his partner. And that makes for a bond that can be even stronger than love.

Hill Street Blues is about more than the fraternity of policemen. It's about a whole police precinct. Set in Anycity, U.S.A., it shows the cops, the lawyers, the criminals, the street people, the merchants, and the visitors in an inner-city area. With its huge cast of regular characters, it does a remarkable job of combining realism and excitement. That's not surprising, though — the producers are the same people who have brought us *The White Shadow, Lou Grant,* and *The Mary Tyler Moore Show.*

Michael Warren

Michael Warren's character, Officer Bobby Hill, knows how to keep his cool. That's very good, especially since his partner, Officer Andy Renko, bears a strong resemblance to a walking volcano.

Michael got his own training in quick, cool thinking as captain of the UCLA Bruins. In 1967 and 1968, he led his team to collegiate basketball championships. Being a star basketball player helped him to get roles in basketball stories — the feature films *Drive, He Said* and *Fast Break* and the TV series *The White Shadow*. Michael's also had parts in *Butterflies Are Free, Marcus Welby, M.D., Police Story, Paris,* and *Lou Grant*. In 1974, he was co-star of the *Sierra* series, in which he played a park ranger.

Michael likes photography, jazz and rhythm-and-blues music, and spending time with his family. He and his wife, Susie, have two children — a girl, Koa, and a boy, Cash.

Charles Haid

Many of Charles Haid's TV roles have been bad guys. But his tough, blustery Officer Renko uses his energy and anger to be one of the best cops on the force. Haid used his own energy as a bouncer, a bartender, and a bricklayer before becoming a professional actor. He was associate producer of *Godspell*, and he appeared in the pilot for the *Barney Miller* series. He had regular TV roles on *Kate McShane*, with Anne Meara, and *Delvecchio*, with Judd Hirsch. (Michael Conrad, Sergeant Phil Esterhaus on *Hill Street Blues*, was another regular on *Delvecchio*.) Haid was co-producer of the TV special *Who Are the DeBolts . . . And Why Do They Have 19 Kids?*

Energetic on his own time, too, Haid sails, fishes, skis, surfs, plays softball, and spends time with his wife, Penelope. He just made a TV movie called *Divorce Wars*, and he'll star this spring in the PBS Playhouse musical, *Working* (based on the book by Studs Terkel).

Bruce Weitz

Mick Belker is not like any TV cop you've ever seen before. Here's an example: Assigned as a decoy to try and trap a rapist, Mick was handed a nurse's outfit to use as a disguise. All dressed up, including a wig and stockings, he looked real cute — even though he *did* refuse to shave off his bushy moustache . . .

No one tried to force him. Mick's got a temper. Set him off, and he may grab your shirt and call you "Hairball." Really get him mad, and he may bite.

In real life, Bruce Weitz is more civilized. He has a solid background of stage performing, and he's been working in television since 1977. Bruce plays racquetball, cooks Chinese food, and weaves throw rugs in his free time. He is married to actress Cecilia Hart.

Write to the stars of *Hill Street Blues* at:

Hill Street Blues
℅ MTM Enterprises
4024 Radford Avenue
Studio City, CA 91604

SHORT TAKES

Alex Handris has had a hard life on *One Day at a Time* (CBS). First his parents were divorced. A year later, his father died. Thirteen-year-old **Glenn Scarpelli** is handling it, though. His portrayal of Alex is helping to keep *One Day at a Time* going strong. Glenn started acting on Broadway when he was nine. He has played opposite Anne Bancroft and Al Pacino, and he also appeared on stage in *Peter Pan* and *Pippin*. He enjoys attending plays when he's not in them. A New York Yankees fan, Glenn spends free time swimming and caring for his pet hamster, Godzilla.

Former Los Angeles Rams defensive lineman, sportscaster, and schoolteacher Jonathan Garvey on *Little House on the Prairie*, **Merlin Olsen** became *Father Murphy* (NBC) this fall. Created by Michael Landon — who also helped create *Little House — Father Murphy* is about a gold miner in the 1870s, who suddenly decides to open an orphanage. Olsen is a descendant of storyteller Hans Christian Andersen. He knows almost firsthand about the old West from the stories of his grandmother, who was born in a covered wagon while her family pioneered through Utah.

A firefighter is some kind of hero to face the dangers of out-of-control blazes. Chris Rorchek on ABC's *Code Red* is played by **Sam J. Jones,** who was some kind of hero once before, when he played Flash Gordon in the movies. Sam got *that* job as a result of appearing as a contestant on *The Dating Game*. (But he didn't get the date.)

———

Adam Rich didn't have much of a vacation after *Eight is Enough* was cancelled as a regular series. He quickly got the part of Danny Blake on *Code Red*. Part of Adam's job now is helping to teach audiences about fire safety, fire prevention, and life-saving techniques.

———

Gabe Kaplan emerged from the reruns of *Welcome Back Kotter* to star in *Lewis and Clark* (NBC) this fall. Like many performers, his first love was sports. Sidetracked from a baseball career by a shoulder injury, Gabe went to work in a New Jersey resort hotel. Watching the entertainers every night, he found his new direction. He started preparing comedy material and worked his way up from small clubs to national television. Since *Welcome Back Kotter*, he's been appearing on TV talk shows and serving as honorary chairman for the Cystic Fibrosis Foundation.

———

After playing six million dollar man Steve Austin, could **Lee Majors** play a TV character with a boring job? Of course not! That's why he chose the role of Colt Seavers, a Hollywood stuntman *and* a bounty hunter on *The Fall Guy* (ABC). Always in tip-top shape, Lee started his career as a football coach. One of his first jobs was assistant playground director for the Los Angeles Parks and Recreation Department. He had a chance to meet a lot of actors at the parks. They gave him the idea to try acting himself. He's starred in several hit series, including *The Big Valley, The Man from Shiloh, Owen Marshall: Counselor at Law,* and, of course, *The Six Million Dollar Man.*

Best friends Zac and Leo on *Mr. Merlin* (CBS) are best friends in real life. **Clark Brandon** and **Jonathan Prince** met in sixth grade. They still write music and play basketball together. Clark guest-starred last season on *The Facts of Life,* where he played Jo's boyfriend, Eddie. His first regular series was *The Fitzpatricks,* and his second was *Out of the Blue.* Jonathan had his first directing job in junior high school, with *West Side Story.* He appeared in the movies *The Incredible Shrinking Woman* and *Halloween II.* His TV roles include *The Secrets of Midland Heights* and the TV movie *Pray TV,* with John Ritter.

Meeno Peluce of ABC's *Best of the West* was born in Amsterdam, Holland. He's lived in the Himalaya mountains of India, and he's been in the United States since he was four years old. Meeno got his first role on an episode of *Starsky and Hutch,* when he was seven. He's been working steadily ever since, including roles on *Eight is Enough* and in the TV movie *Scout's Honor.* Meeno is interested in sports, music, marine biology, and architecture. He's already a film producer — 8mm only.

Nell Carter has been singing since she was six years old. That's not a talent called for in her most recent TV series, *Gimme A Break* (NBC), about a housekeeper and the family she works for. Nell sang in her local Presbyterian church in

Birmingham, Alabama; in New York City nightclubs; on Broadway; and in the TV special *Baryshnikov on Broadway*. She starred as Sgt. Hildy Jones on NBC's *Lobo* last season.

Jameson Parker and **Gerald McRaney** (A.J. and Rick on CBS's *Simon and Simon*) both got into acting partly because of leg injuries. Jameson moved from Wisconsin to Washington, D.C., for a knee operation while he was in college. (He was already studying drama.) He wound up getting a job with a production of *The Great White Hope* and did two other shows there. Gerald had to find an activity to replace football after he broke his leg in junior high school. His sister suggested trying out for a local college play. He did and discovered he loved acting.

Garin Bougie of *Maggie* (ABC) is in tenth grade this year. He started acting — in school plays — when he was eight. Garin takes acting classes along with his regular studies, but he's not sure performing will be his final career. He's also thinking about writing, directing, and running his own business. Garin appeared last season in the TV movie *Children of Divorce*.

Dana Hill is just as good in drama as she is in comedy. Dana plays Gabby Gallagher on CBS's *The Two of Us,* with Peter Cook and Mimi Kennedy. She had the very serious leading role in *Fallen Angel* last year, and she also appeared with Linda Lavin in *The $5.20 an Hour Dream*. When she's not acting, Dana likes to participate in all kinds of sports.

James Garner and **Stuart Margolin,** who teamed up in *The Rockford Files*, came together again this fall for *Bret Maverick* (NBC). Garner didn't have to spend a lot of time getting to know his character. He played the gambling, reluçtant gunslinger Maverick on TV from 1957 to 1960. It was his first major TV role. Margolin co-starred with Garner once before, in a series called *Nichols,* and they appear together in the new TV movie *Hangin' On.*

_____

Randy Hamilton stars in two different network shows this year — on two different networks! Randy plays Rikki Dekker on the NBC daytime drama *Texas.* He is also the new host of ABC's *Kids Are People, Too.* Randy is a singer, and he gets to use his talent on both shows. A native of Ohio, Randy now lives in New York. He enjoys music — jazz, rock, rhythm and blues — and sports, especially football and baseball.

_____